ABOUT

QUANTUM

BOOKS

QUANTUM, THE UNIT OF
EMITTED ENERGY. A QUANTUM
BOOK IS A SHORT STUDY
DISTINCTIVE FOR THE AUTHOR'S
ABILITY TO OFFER A RICHNESS OF
DETAIL AND INSIGHT WITHIN
ABOUT ONE HUNDRED PAGES
OF PRINT. SHORT ENOUGH TO BE
READ IN AN EVENING AND
SIGNIFICANT ENOUGH
TO BE A BOOK.

THE ILLUSION OF POWER

Stephen Orgel

The Illusion of Power

Political Theater in the

English Renaissance

University of California Press

Berkeley, Los Angeles, London

University of California Press
Berkeley and Los Angeles, California

University of California Press, Ltd.
London, England

To my mother and father

Contents

Illustrations

Preface

This book extends and develops certain ideas in my *Inigo Jones* (London and Berkeley, 1973), written in collaboration with Roy Strong, and therefore necessarily covers some of the same material. I have tried to keep annotation to a minimum; sources, detailed documentation, and background will all be found in *Inigo Jones,* as will the complete texts of the court productions cited here.

It is a pleasure to acknowledge first my debt to many discussions with Roy Strong over the four years of our collaboration. David Kalstone, Edmund White, Stephen Greenblatt, Alice Daniel, and A. J. Sherman have been acute and encouraging critics. My attention was called to the description of the Cambridge *Aulularia* by Robert J. Meyer, and to Bacon's passage on royal science by Peter Carlson, two exemplary students. The engravings of the Teatro Olimpico were kindly supplied by George Starr. The photographs of the Inigo Jones drawings were provided by the Courtauld Institute and the Westerham Press, and are reproduced by permission of the Trustees of the Chatsworth settlement.

1

Theaters and Audiences

This is an essay about theater at court. It takes as its examples certain particular instances in the Renaissance in England, where the phenomenon was specially important and heavily subsidized; but the general implications of the argument extend beyond a specific place and historical moment.

Court theaters were always radically different from public theaters, not only in the nature of their audiences, but in the status they conferred upon their actors and the significance of the theatrical experiences they presented. In the public world of Renaissance Europe (and indeed, for three centuries after in varying degrees) actors were traditionally considered itinerants, a step above beggars and highwaymen. In the court world, the same actors became Gentlemen, the King's Servants, or the Queen's Men.

James Burbage built his theater outside London in 1576; this was either the first or the second permanent theater in Europe after Roman times, and both its priority and its uniqueness were asserted in its very name:

The Theater.[1] For the profession of acting, this was a significant move toward social respectability, though doubtless Burbage's primary motivation was financial; but its ancillary effects involved more than respectability or security. Before this moment, the concept of theater had included no sense of *place*. A theater was not a building, it was a group of actors and an audience; the theater was any place in which they chose to perform. When the play was over, the hall or courtyard or banqueting room ceased to be a theater.

The fact that in a particular brief period—twenty years or so—this concept became located and embodied in architecture tells us something important about the requirements of Renaissance culture and its changing view of itself. All at once theater was an institution, a property, a corporation. For the first time in more than a thousand years it had the sort of reality that meant most to Renaissance society: it was *real* in the way that "real estate" is real; it was a location, a building, a possession—an established and visible part of society. And having a permanent place, it also had a regular attendance, a permanent audience: theaters create not only their dramas, but their audiences as well.

I wish to begin by considering the nature and implications of the new playhouse, for this building was the physical embodiment of both an idea of theater and an idea of the society it was created to entertain. Figure 1 shows the closest thing we possess to a contemporary

[1] There are references to a permanent theatrical structure of some sort in Ferrara before 1550. See A. d'Ancona, *Origini del Teatro Italiano* (Turin, 1891), 2:137.

FIGURE 1. *Arend van Buchel after Johannes de Witt. The Swan Theater, c. 1596. (University of Utrecht Library)*

drawing of the interior of an Elizabethan theater. This
is a playhouse called the Swan, built in 1596. In that
year or shortly afterward a Dutch traveler named Johannes de Witt visited London and was particularly
impressed with the theaters. He described them in a
letter to his friend Arend van Buchel of Utrecht; the
Swan especially interested de Witt because it seemed to
him to be based on a Roman model, and he included
a drawing of it, labeling the parts of the building with
Roman theatrical terms derived from Vitruvius, the
great Augustan codifier of classical architecture. The
letter and drawing have disappeared, but van Buchel
copied them into his journal, and this has survived.
There is, of course, no way of knowing whether or how
van Buchel altered de Witt's original, and there are
certain puzzling details in the drawing; but it remains
a prime piece of evidence about the Elizabethan theater
—indeed, we have only two other views of the interiors
of public playhouses before the Restoration.

De Witt's drawing shows a simple platform stage
with no scenery and minimal properties, a back façade
with two entrances, a gallery above, two elegant columns supporting a floor over the gallery. A scene is in
progress, but the only spectators visible are in the gallery. This is one of the puzzling details, since the gallery
in Elizabethan theaters was a playing area, and there
is no other evidence that seats were sold there. On the
other hand, it is apparent from the openness of the
stage that no rigid separation existed between actors and
spectators at such a theater, and it may be that the gallery was indeed used from time to time to accommo-

date members of the audience. De Witt's letter adds the information that the Swan was the largest and most splendid of the London public playhouses, that it was built of flint, with columns painted to look like marble, and had a capacity of three thousand.

The theater depicted here has little provision for scenery. One may use props in it, but no settings more complex than a backdrop hung from the gallery, and, because of the placement of the audience, nothing requiring scenic perspective. The building is primarily an auditorium, designed for speeches and gesture; acting in it will be largely a form of oratory. We know that Elizabethan playhouses had a certain amount of machinery—trapdoors in the stage and in the roof above the stage, winches for descents of deities, thunder machines and exploding devices, and the like—but essentially they were theaters not of settings and scenic machines, not of illusions, but of actors. We know too that despite the minimal scenery, productions could be very splendid, with enormous emphasis on costume and pageantry. Indeed, the costumes were real court garments, as Thomas Platter, a Swiss visitor in 1599, observed: "The comedians are very expensively and elegantly costumed, since it is usual in England, when important gentlemen or knights die, for their finest clothes to be bequeathed to their servants, and since it is not proper for them to wear such clothes, instead they subsequently give them to the comedians to purchase very cheaply." [2] This means that when the or-

[2] The original (with an inaccurate translation) is in E. K. Chambers, *The Elizabethan Stage* (Oxford, 1923), 2:364.

dinary Elizabethan went to the theater to see a play about royalty, he might have thought of the drama as a mere fiction, but its trappings were paradoxically the real thing.

There are crucial differences between a playhouse such as this and a court or private theater. The public playhouse is built by producers and theatrical entrepreneurs, the directors of theatrical companies, and its audience is their creation. The public theater will be successful only to the extent that individual citizens, potential spectators, are willing to compose themselves into that audience the producers have imagined. But private theaters are the creation of their audiences, and are often designed not only for a particular group but for a particular production or occasion.[3] Two of the earliest theaters in Italy are cases in point: the Teatro Olimpico in Vicenza was built by Palladio and Scamozzi for the city's Olympic Academy, specifically for a production of *Oedipus;* the Teatro degli Uffizi in Florence was created by Buontalenti for a group of spectacular performances celebrating the wedding of Ferdinando de' Medici. In England the court playhouse—the building itself—was a late and relatively insignificant adjunct to the life of Whitehall. There was a small theater attached to the palace, called the Cockpit-in-Court, but

[3] I am using the term "private" here to refer to a playhouse commissioned by and created for a particular person or group, not to theaters like the Blackfriars, which are usually described as "private" because they were technically private houses, and therefore not subject to City regulations. The Blackfriars was as "public" as the Globe, in the sense that anyone who paid the price of admission could attend.

the really important productions took place not there
but in the central areas of the court itself: the Great
Hall, the Banqueting House. In the world of the court,
such theatricals were, like the other events that took
place in the Hall and the Banqueting House, celebrations of royal power and assertions of aristocratic community.

Indeed, architectural theorists in the Renaissance considered the adaptability of palace halls to stage productions as an essential part of their design—that is,
considered theatrical performances to be an essential
element in the life of a court. And for Sebastiano Serlio,
the most important interpreter of Vitruvian principles
before Palladio, the lavishness of court productions took
on a significant social and political role, for it was a
measure of the magnanimity and liberality of princes:

> The more such things cost, the more they are esteemed, for
> they are things which stately and great persons doe, which
> are enemies to niggardlinesse. This have I seene in some
> Scenes made by Ieronimo Genga, for the pleasure and
> delight of his lord and patron Francisco Maria, Duke of
> Urbin: wherein I saw so great liberalitie used by the Prince,
> and so good a conceit in the workeman, and so good Art
> and proportion in things therein represented, as ever I saw
> in all my life before. Oh good Lord, what magnificence was
> there to be seene . . . but I leave all these things to the dis-
> cretion and consideration of the judicious workeman; which
> shall make all such things as their pattrons serve them,
> which they must worke after their owne devises, and never
> take care what it shall cost.[4]

[4] From the first English translation of the *Architettura* 1611.
See Stephen Orgel and Roy Strong, *Inigo Jones* (Berkeley,
1973), 1:6.

Dramas at court were not entertainments in the simple and dismissive sense we usually apply to the term. They were expressions of the age's most profound assumptions about the monarchy. They included strong elements of ritual and communion, often explicitly religious; and to participate in such a production involved far more than simply watching a play. A Whitehall audience was qualitatively different from an audience at the Globe or the Blackfriars. The Elizabethan public theater established a hierarchy that was primarily economic, though of course it had intellectual and social implications as well. Spectators paid a penny to enter and stand; for another penny they had seats in the gallery; for a third penny they had front row seats; for a shilling they had a gentleman's or lord's room, a private box. Within these categories all spectators were equal; nothing in the structure of the playhouse or the quality of the theatrical experience distinguished the lord who paid his threepence from the merchant who paid his.

In this respect the public theater may be seen as a democratizing institution, though to put it in those terms is a little misleading: its appeal was primarily to the middle class. A penny was a day's wages for the average workman, so one had to be reasonably well off to go to the theater at all, and relatively prosperous to attend regularly and sit comfortably. Whatever aesthetic requirements Elizabethan drama fulfilled, a large part of the visual appeal of the spectacles was surely directed toward satisfying middle-class aspirations. The costumes, we have seen, were real court clothes, and their splendor, in a society whose sumptuary laws regulated even styles of dress, would have given a merchant or tradesman the richest sense he was ever likely to have of how the aristocratic life looked in action.

This was the audience that the King's Men played to when they played at the Globe. But when the king brought his players to court the nature of the audience changed, as, often, did the function of the performance. Now there were, properly speaking, two audiences and two spectacles. The primary audience was the monarch, and the performance was often directed explicitly at him. Thus, early in Queen Elizabeth's reign two political theorists gave the young queen counsel through the dramatic example of *Gorboduc;* and later, in *The Arraignment of Paris,* a poet created for her a crucial role in the mythology of the commonwealth. At these performances what the rest of the spectators watched was not a play but the queen at a play, and their response would have been not simply to the drama, but to the relationship between the drama and its primary audience, the royal spectator.

An account of a Cambridge production in 1564 reveals precisely how essential a part of the spectacle the queen was. The play was Plautus' *Aulularia,* and the performance was in King's College chapel:

> For the hearing and playing whereof, was made by her
> Highnes surveyor and at her own cost, in the body of the
> Church, a great stage containing the breadth of the church
> from one side to the other, that the chapels might serve for
> houses. . . . Upon the south-wall was hanged a cloth of
> state, with the appurtenances and half-pace [dais] for her

Majesty. In the rood-loft, another stage for ladies and
gentlewomen to stand on. And the two lower tables under
the said rood-loft, were greatly enlarged and rayled for the
choyce officers of the Court. . . . When all things were
ready for the plays, the Lord Chamberlayn with Mr Secretary came in; bringing a multitude of the guard with them
having every man in his hand a torch-staff, for the lights
of the play. . . . From the quire doore unto the stage was
made as 'twere a bridge rayled on both sides; for the Queen's
Grace to go to the stage. . . . At last her Highness came,
with certain Lords, Ladies, and Gentlewomen: all the Pen-
sioners going on both sides, with torch staves . . . and so
took her seat, and heard the play fully.[5]

The royal seat, that is, was placed directly on the
stage. There are a number of similar examples, though
of course this may not have been the only method of
staging a play at Elizabeth's court. But it should lead us
to entertain the possibility that when the queen concluded *The Arraignment of Paris* by receiving the
golden apple from Paris's hand, or when she settled the
contentions of *Every Man Out of his Humor,* she did so
from the stage and as part of the action. After 1605,
when perspective settings were introduced—and they
were used *only* at court or when royalty was present—
the monarch became the center of the theatrical experience in another way, and the aristocratic hierarchy grew
even more apparent. In a theater employing perspective, there is only one focal point, one perfect place in
the hall from which the illusion achieves its fullest effect. At court performances this is where the king sat,

---

[5] Quoted by Glynne Wickham, *Early English Stages* (London, 1963), 1:249–250.

and the audience around him at once became a living emblem of the structure of the court. The closer one sat to the monarch the "better" one's place was, an index to one's status, and more directly, to the degree of favor one enjoyed. Ambassadorial disputes frequently hinged on whether sufficient honor had been conferred upon a particular legation by its placement at the Christmas masque. James I found that an easy way to insult the Venetians was to seat them farther than the Spaniards from the royal box. The theater thus became, in the most direct way, a political entity as well.

Here, for comparison, is a private theater designed for a society of equals. Figure 2 shows the stage of the Teatro Olimpico, designed by Andrea Palladio for the Olympic Academy in Vicenza, of which he was a founding member. The academy consisted of sixty-three elected fellows, and was devoted to classical studies, particularly of drama. It sponsored regular productions of ancient and neoclassic plays, and the architect created for it a theater based on the Vitruvian model. After Palladio's death in 1580 the building was completed by Vincenzo Scamozzi, who added to the stage façade five extraordinary perspective street scenes. Figure 3 is a floor plan of the theater. The hall is elliptical, and the perspectives run back from the stage façade along the radii of the ellipse. As in the royal productions at Whitehall, it is perspective that defines the audience. At court, only the king has a perfect seat. But *every* spectator in this amphitheater views one (and only one) perfect perspective.

The central experience of drama at court, then, in-

FIGURE 2. *A. Palladio and V. Scamozzi. Teatro Olimpico, Vicenza: stage façade. (Engraving by*

V. Brunello, from Le Piante e Prospetti d'Architettura di Palladio, *Vicenza, 1818.*)

volved not simply the action of a play, but the interaction between the play and the monarch, and the structured organization of the other spectators around him. This assertion does not describe a tacit assumption or a metaphysical conceit; it describes an emphatic practical requirement, which, when scanted, produced objections that were explicit, immediate, and severe. For example, in 1605 King James paid a visit to Oxford, and the university undertook to entertain him with four plays. A stage was constructed in Christ Church hall, and for the first time in England drama was produced with perspective sets and movable scenery; the designer was Inigo Jones. The location of the royal seat was determined by the laws of optics. However, according to a contemporary account, when representatives arrived from court to oversee the arrangements for the performances, they "utterly disliked the stage at Christ Church, and above all, the place appointed for the chair of Estate, because it was no higher, and the King so placed that the auditory could see but his cheek only." The university's vice-chancellor undertook to explain "that by the art perspective the King should behold all better than if he sat higher." But the courtiers remained adamant, and "in the end, the place was removed, and sett in the midst of the Hall, but too far from the stage." Ironically, the problem turned out in the end to be acoustical rather than optical, and the king complained that he could not hear the play.[6]

What troubles the courtiers in this account is that the

[6] The full account is reprinted and discussed in *Inigo Jones,* 1:6–8, and 2:823–826.

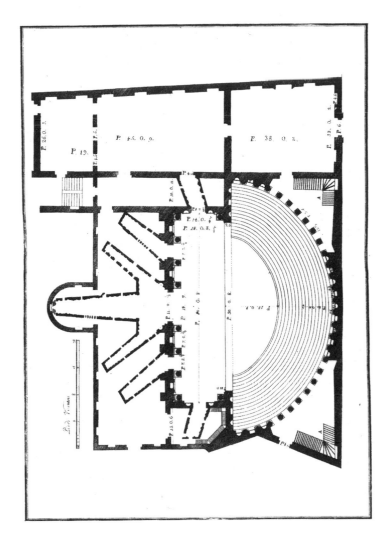

FIGURE 3. *Teatro Olimpico: floor plan.*

king's place in relation to the drama is, in the arrangement of the hall, unclear. The king must not merely see the play, he must be seen to see it. The fact that the latter requirement interferes with the former is of no consequence to the critics from Whitehall; in their judgment, it is the latter that takes clear precedence. Nor should we find this especially surprising; the same assumption has persisted to the present day. During the Regency, the royal boxes at the Drury Lane Theater were the front boxes on either side of the stage, the king's on the left, the regent's on the right. Since the auditorium was designed as a horseshoe, both boxes were especially poor places from which to see the spectacle, but both were in full view of every other seat in the house. Only opera houses, created for the most aristocratic and least democratic of theatrical forms, have been able to afford to give their royal boxes a central location: they are placed at the midpoint of the first gallery. When the queen goes to Covent Garden, she is symbolically seated in the center of the tier of the most privileged spectators. But even this spot is too far from the stage to provide the royal viewer with a really good seat; there are many better places from which to see the opera. The virtue of the center box is, even today, its full view not of the stage but of the audience.

There is another important aspect to the account of the productions at Christ Church in 1605. The courtiers refer to the spectators as an "auditory." What this audience has come to *see* is the king; but their experience of the drama will be—as the terms *auditory* and *audience* suggest—to hear it. Theater in 1605 was assumed to be a verbal medium. And acting, we have seen, was a form of oratory; the Renaissance actor did not merely imitate action, he persuaded the audience through speech and gesture of the meaning of the action. Obviously much more than this was in fact being experienced in an Elizabethan theater for example pageantry, violence, symbolism—for which the visual sense was essential. But this did not render the drama any less a verbal form. Modern theatrical historians frequently confuse the issue by treating the verbal and the spectacular as antithetical kinds of theater. In this line of argument, court theaters, with their movable settings and marvelous machines, become the culprits that destroyed the golden age of Shakespearean drama by creating and catering to a vulgar taste for shows. Theater thus became a visual medium, and the era of poetic drama was ended.

This is an attractive thesis largely because our own sense of theater is so intensely visual. In producing a play, we begin by extinguishing the house lights, so that the only visible part of the theater is the stage; we assume that the primary way to control an audience's attention is through its eyes. And, a logical corollary, we always say we are going to *see* a play, never to hear it. But all this is much newer than the seventeenth century. Until the late nineteenth century it was usual to perform plays with uniform lighting throughout the theater; there are occasional counter-examples, but they are exceptional. The darkened house and the lighted stage are elements in a specifically modern concept of theater; its *avant garde* includes Wagner at Bayreuth

and Sir Henry Irving. Until the end of the last century
it was perfectly possible to say that one went to *hear*
a play—Henry James, reviewing the Paris theatrical sea-
son of 1872 said he had gone "to the Théâtre Français
to listen to Molière's *Mariage Forcé*." [7] This would be
for us an impossible locution, though again, opera re-
tains more of the older tradition than drama: we are
still as likely to say we went to hear *Don Giovanni* as
to say we went to see it.

Viewed from a Renaissance standpoint, the antithesis between verbal and visual theater looks very different. The drama, from Aristotle onward, had always
been a branch of poetry. It need not have been. Aristotle could have seen it as an extension of some visually
oriented form such as dance, thereby confirming a very
ancient anthropological theory about the theater's ori-
gin. But the treatise on drama is called the *Poetics,*
not the *Choreographics.* Drama differs from other
forms of poetry, however, in that it is designed to be
seen as well as heard. Renaissance critics put it this
way: the *mode of expression,* or the *means* of drama,
was spectacle. They included in the term *spectacle* everything one saw on the stage, from the mere appearance
of the characters to the most elaborate kinds of scenic
machinery. For purists this quality of drama was not a
point in its favor; it rendered the art a lower kind of
poetry than, say, epic. But the fact that spectacle was
essential to it did not make drama any the less a form
of poetry.

[7] Allan Wade, ed., *The Scenic Art* (New Brunswick, 1948),
p. 4.

The distinction, then, between "verbal" theaters and "visual" theaters in this period is a false one. Both the Globe and the court theater were spectacular, both were highly rhetorical; the visual and the verbal emphases in no way excluded each other. In fact, if we look at plays that were specifically written to be produced with scenes and machines, we shall find them far more elaborately rhetorical than plays for the public stage. One example may suffice. In 1634 Henrietta Maria commissioned from a courtier named Walter Montagu a pastoral in which she and her ladies could perform on a stage designed by Inigo Jones. The result was *The Shepherd's Paradise,* a series of debates about a topic dear to the queen's heart, Platonic love. It was produced in a setting that changed nine times, and lasted almost eight hours. The difference between this sort of theater and the popular stage is obviously not to be found in any antithesis between the spectacular and the verbal, but rather in the *kind* of experience the two theaters provided, and the underlying assumptions they made about their audiences.

Let us begin with what is presented in a theater, the action of a drama. In a popular playhouse action was perceived on an open stage extending out into the audience. Nothing but the height of the stage separated the actor from the spectator at the Globe. Whereas in a modern theater the audience is assumed to be an unseen spectator, overhearing the dialogue, in the Elizabethan playhouse he was addressed directly and constantly. Burbage's Hamlet did not ruminate his way through his soliloquies, he harangued, exhorted, explained. As at a debate or oration, in the audience's judgment lay half the action.

Here we must beware of the easy antithesis between verbal and spectacular theaters: the court theater, with its scenes and machines, did not diminish the oratorical aspects of the drama, but rather intensified them. *The Shepherd's Paradise* is an extreme but not uncharacteristic case. The queen saw in plays a didactic medium, a forum in which her philosophical position might be thoroughly argued. Why such a drama should have been performed with scenes at all is an important question, and one I shall return to; but here I wish only to consider the effect of the scenes on the action. To begin with, perspective settings require a proscenium, a frame at the front of the stage—Montagu's audience was separated from his actors in a way that the popular dramatist's was not. But a frame does more than separate the viewer from the scene. It also directs his attention and provides a context for the action it contains. The context, moreover, need not be related to the action within the frame. An elaborate gold frame around a painting says something quite different from a simple black band, but what it says is about its owner, not about the painting. A framed painting differs, too, from an unframed one, such as a fresco. The fresco is designed for a particular person in a particular place; it extends his life outward into heroic or pastoral vistas that include the architecture of his home. It can be repainted or destroyed, but it cannot, except with enormous difficulty, be removed; and if it is removed it will be, literally, out of place. But paintings are portable, and what is more, marketable. The frame—the great gilt masterpiece, an entity separate from the picture, created by the framer, not by the artist—comes into being when paintings become commodities, objects to be bought and collected. Thus paintings are framed in gold not because gold has anything to do with the particular picture, but because paintings are valuable; the frame objectifies and symbolizes the investment. A framed painting is possessed, limited, defined; and what it depicts becomes an epitome, life in miniature and under control.

So it is with a framed stage, the theater created and possessed by its audience. Renaissance proscenium arches, too, did not merely enclose the action. They were designed for particular occasions, and often in very complex ways defined the worlds of both their patrons and their dramatic fictions. For example, the proscenium of *The Shepherd's Paradise* (Figure 4) consisted of two pilasters with crouching captives, one on either side; above them shields, the left displaying a burning heart, the right an open eye; above these Roman armor suspended from lions' heads. Across the top ran a Doric frieze, with a goatskin in the middle inscribed *The Shepherd's Paradise.* Here, for the court spectator, Caroline royal philosophy was mysteriously epitomized. The captives and armor embody its heroic theme of the subjugation of the passions, represented by the lions; the flaming heart of love is juxtaposed against the vigilant eye of reason; surmounting all this action and passion is the noble simplicity of the Doric order and the peaceful pastoral symbol of the goatskin.

FIGURE 4. The Shepherd's Paradise: *proscenium and standing scene. (Devonshire Collection, Chatsworth.*

The Inigo Jones drawings are in this collection, unless otherwise indicated.)

Within this dark conceit the dramatic action unfolded.
How did action unfold on a Renaissance stage? In
the public theater, through dialogue, movement and
gesture, pageantry and symbolism. These functioned as
a unit; little that was expressed in action did not have
its concomitant rhetoric, few symbols went unexplained
by language. In this respect the drama resembled the
other visual arts in the Renaissance: every painting—
even a portrait—had its moral or allegorical meaning;
every emblem had its motto; the architectural orders
had their significances; even nature, God's great arti-
fact, could be conceived as a book. We tend to slight
the Renaissance pressure toward *explanation*, stressing
instead the age's devotion to symbolic modes of expression. But again, the verbal was inseparable from the visual. Then as now, a symbol had meaning only after it
was explained. Symbols function as summations and
confirmations; they tell us only what we already know,
and it is a mistake to assume that the Renaissance audience, unlike a modern one, knew without being told.
Even emblems that seem perfectly obvious, or those
that derive from standard handbooks of symbolic imagery, were relentlessly explicated. There was, of course,
an alternative pleasure to be derived from mysteries
and enigmas, and symbols were often left unexplained
to emphasize the occult aspects of poetic wisdom. But
in such cases, to all except the most iconographically
sophisticated, they remained enigmatic, and the artist
was relying not on the observer's ability to interpret the
symbolism, but precisely on his inability to do so.
Obscurantism was not, however, the usual intention of
Renaissance imagery; emblems were always accom-

panied by their explanatory poems,[8] devices by their
mottoes. So at the theater, when Shakespeare introduced Rumor as the Chorus to *The Second Part of
Henry the Fourth,* he dressed him in the full parapher-
nalia of a Renaissance iconographer, a costume "painted
full of tongues," which he then carefully elucidated:

> Open your ears; for which of you will stop
> The vent of hearing when loud Rumor speaks?
> I, from the orient to the drooping west,
> Making the wind my post-horse, still unfold
> The acts commenced on this ball of earth.
> Upon my tongues continual slanders ride. . . .

When Ben Jonson opened *The Masque of Beauty*
with Boreas (the north wind) and January, he gave
them the attributes he found in the standard Renaissance *Iconology* of Cesare Ripa. Boreas had a rough
beard and grey wings, his feet ended in serpents' tails,
and he carried a leafless branch covered with icicles.
January sat on a silver throne, wore an ash-colored robe
fringed with silver, a white mantle and a laurel wreath,
had white wings, and carried a laurel bough. Commen-
tators since Burckhardt have assured us that the Renaissance spectator would have recognized these figures at
once. Jonson apparently believed otherwise, for however standard the imagery, January begins the masque
by explaining it:

> I too well know thee
> By thy rude voice that doth so hoarsely blow,
> Thy hair, thy beard, thy hills o'er-hilled with snow,

---

[8] Indeed, strictly speaking, the emblem was only the poem,
and the picture was merely illustrative. See S. Orgel, "Affecting
the Metaphysics," *Harvard English Studies,* 2 (1971):233.

Thy serpent feet, to be that rough north wind,
Boreas, that to my reign art still unkind.
I am the prince of months called January. . . .

But dialogue is more than explication. One of our chief difficulties in producing Elizabethan plays on modern stages is the ubiquitousness of the dialogue; it does not only explain, it often parallels or duplicates the action. Even in the heat of combat, Renaissance characters regularly pause to describe in words the actions we see taking place. Modern plays rely far less heavily on dialogue, and a great deal of the dramatist's text—stage directions, accounts of the settings, and the like—are realized for an audience not through the actor's language at all, but exclusively through the art of the director and designer. In the Elizabethan public theater, however, nothing spoke for itself; every action implied a rhetoric.

We should logically ask next what happened when a play from the public theater was produced with scenic machinery, but the question is misleading. Illusionistic stages were used, on the whole, not for drama but for the masque, for reasons we shall consider in the next chapter. Plays from the popular playhouses were frequently performed at court, but never with settings.[9]

[9] There were apparently only two exceptions before the closing of the theaters in 1642. In January 1634, a year after *The Shepherd's Paradise,* Jones's costumes, and presumably the scenery too, were used again for a court revival of Fletcher's *Faithful Shepherdess;* and in November, Jones designed sets for a court performance of Heywood's *Love's Mistress,* which the king and queen had seen at the Phoenix a week before. These were anomalous instances, and in any case we have no information about how they were staged.

On the other hand, plays written specifically for royal productions often had scenery, and by the 1630s were expected to do so. We possess detailed information about the staging of only one such play, an anonymous French pastoral called *Florimène,* produced in 1635, and performed by Queen Henrietta Maria's French maids of honor. What has survived of this work is not a text, but something much more valuable for our purposes: an English summary of the action, Inigo Jones's plans and elevations of the stage and the arrangement of the hall, and a complete set of scene designs. This constitutes a unique piece of primary evidence about the nature of theater at court, and may therefore serve us as a guide for assessing the effects of the new stage upon the drama.

Jones set up his stage in the Great Hall of Whitehall Palace. Here is his diagram of the arrangement of the room (Figure 5). Let us look first at the audience. The spectators are ranged in boxes and tiers around three walls of the room. The royal box is exactly halfway between the front of the stage and the back wall of the hall—the king and queen sit in the precise center of the audience. The area in front of the royal box is clear; no one has his back to the monarchs, no one sits in front of them. The location of four particular boxes is also indicated. The best, those directly behind the thrones to the right and left, are assigned to the Countess of Arundel, wife of the famous collector who was instrumental in the creation of the king's own art collection, and to an unnamed marchioness. Close to the stage is a box for Sir Thomas Edmondes, a distinguished dip-

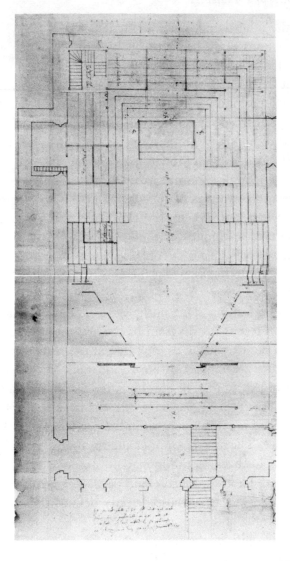

FIGURE 5. Florimène: *plan of the stage and hall.*
(*British Museum*)

lomat, former ambassador to Brussels and Paris, and
royalist MP—but not an aristocrat, hence his distance
from the throne. And Inigo Jones's own box, labeled
"master surveyor," is in the top two tiers on the king's
right.

Now let us look at the stage. It is constructed in two
parts. The front section consists of the proscenium arch
and four angled side wings. This is a "standing scene";
that is, it did not change during the course of the play.
But behind this is a very different kind of setting. First
there are two pairs of shutters; these run in grooves in
the stage, and are shown open. Next come three lines
labeled in Jones's hand "works of Relievo to Remove,"
and finally there is a backdrop. The "works of Relievo,"
or scenes of relieve, were cutouts arranged in layers that
gave an impression of great depth to the rear of a setting. Here they are in three sections; they can be
changed (they are "to Remove"), presumably while the
shutters in front of them are closed. The production of
Florimène included five separate scenes of relieve.

The front part of the stage, then, consisted of a fixed
setting; within this area the actors performed. The back
part, however, was an enormously versatile scenic machine; it underwent a complete transformation seven
times, and an eighth change took place in the heavens
above the rear stage. *Florimène* was in fact one of
Jones's simplest spectacles—it was a rare Christmas
masque at this period that did not include an aerial bal-
let or a vision of the heavenly spheres in motion—but
the basic form of the stage was always as we see it here,
with its clear division between action and scenic de-

vices. The separation of the two areas is revealed even
more vividly by Jones's side elevation (Figure 6). Here
we see the acting area, its stage slightly raked, with
cloud borders hanging above it, and at its back the lines
of the shutters, two below and one above. Behind this
is an inner stage for the scenes of relieve, and above,
three tiers of seats for deities appearing in the clouds.

All this was concealed by a curtain as the audience
took their places. No house lights were dimmed to
begin the performance; the spectators' own costumes
and jewels were part of the show. The curtain rose on
a pastoral landscape, the island of Delos. Here is the
opening scene as Jones designed it (Figure 7). The
drawing shows only the front section of the stage—the
back shutters are closed. The setting is framed by a
proscenium arch depicting shepherdesses with musical
instruments, putti holding garlands and playing games.
This frame is not a barrier between the audience and
the scene: the stage projects beyond it, and a double
stair runs to the floor of the hall. Like most productions
of this sort, *Florimène* concluded with the descent of
the aristocratic performers to lead the court in a grand
ball.

The play opens with the entrance of Fame to speak
a prologue to the king. Its text has not survived, but it
was doubtless a mixture of compliment and explanation. At its conclusion the back shutter parts, revealing,
far within the landscape, the first of the scenes of relieve, a colonnaded temple with a statue of Diana.
Priests appear and sing, shepherds and shepherdesses
offer gifts to the goddess, and join the priests in another

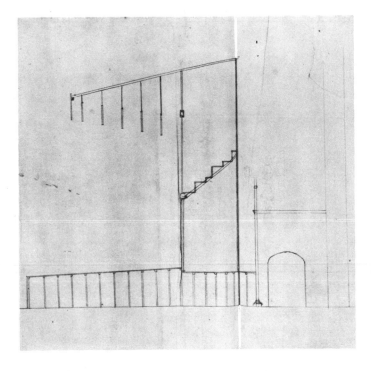

FIGURE 6. Florimène: *side elevation of the stage.*
(*British Museum*)

FIGURE 7. *Inigo Jones.* Florimène: *stage, proscenium, and standing scene.* (*Devonshire Collection, Chatsworth*)

song; the shutter closes, and the stage presents the standing scene once more.

Now the principal characters enter. The plot they enact, despite incredibly tortuous complexities, is perfectly familiar in type. The shepherd Filène falls in love with the shepherdess Florimène, and disguises himself as a woman to gain access to her. The shepherdess Lycoris falls in love with Filène, and disguises herself as a man to gain access to him. The shepherdess Lucinde is in love with the shepherd Aristée, but Aristée has fallen in love with the disguised Filène, and disguises himself as a shepherdess in his turn. And so forth for five acts, until Diana concludes matters by divine fiat, and a chorus of deities appears in the heavens to ratify her wisdom. To an audience raised on romances, the only surprises in this elaborate French charade would have been those provided by Inigo Jones's machinery.

Jones's surprises were real enough. Interestingly, however, they bore very little relation to the action of the drama, taking place, for the most part, only in the intervals between the acts. The text calls these *"intermedii"* [10]—interludes, the Italian *intermezzi*. In fact, throughout the sixteenth century in Italy, this had been the primary function of scenic machinery: not to form a context for dramatic action, but to provide spectacular *intermezzi*. As in *Florimène*, these were normally

[10] Since the singular is *intermedium,* the plural should properly be *intermedia;* however, *intermedii* is the form that regularly appears in texts of the period. The word seems to have been thought of as Latin in the singular, Italian in the plural.

unrelated to the main play. Purists scorned the practice, but many Renaissance theorists defended it, pointing out that Aristotle himself recommended the use of spectacle to produce the wonder that is required in drama. And other critics praised the *intermezzi* on the grounds that they served to mitigate the overwhelming effects of tragedy. No doubt this argument sounds perverse to modern readers—we tend to want our tragedies intensified, not mitigated; but perhaps that is because we start by taking tragedy so much less seriously than the Renaissance spectator did. Even Dr. Johnson, in an age we think of as rationalistic, felt that *King Lear* was more than he could endure, and craved a happy ending.

Jones's use of machinery was strictly traditional, then, and explicable, moreover, in good theoretical terms. Even for plays that did not include formal *intermezzi,* he tended to employ his scenic machines in the same way, to provide brief interludes of wonder. In *Florimène,* in the pauses between the shepherds' and shepherdesses' dialogues of passion, confusion, despair, the distant landscape parted to reveal four elegant tableaux of the seasons, the cycle of the pastoral year. The action of *Florimène,* however, is continuous; nothing in the play's time scheme was being expressed by these scenic marvels. What then did they say to the spectator of 1635? What did the final apotheosis say, the sudden appearance of a full pantheon in Jones's heavens, rendered heroic in size by the stage's diminishing perspective? In part, undoubtedly, that beyond the mere complexities of human behavior a larger life pursues its course, that despite appearances the universe is orderly and providential after all. But the spectator's response would have been to something greater and more immediate as well. For in those interludes, in that apotheosis, and in the many far more elaborate scenic spectacles that Jones annually created, the theater itself became an entity; the stage was not the setting for a drama, but was itself the action. And its transformations were those of the human mind, the imagination expressing itself through perspective, mechanics, the imitation of nature, creating a model of the universe and bringing it under rational control. Such a theater, as we have seen, has little to do with plays; it is, indeed, in certain ways antidramatic. But it proved peculiarly appropriate to the special audience who commanded its creation.

2

The Royal Spectacle

Why did the Renaissance consider perspective settings and spectacular machinery particularly and exclusively appropriate to courts? The question is capable of several kinds of answers; we have already touched on two of them. Illusionistic theaters made of their audiences living emblems of the aristocratic hierarchy, and their costly scenic wonders constituted a prime instance of royal liberality, exemplifying the princely virtue of magnificence. But though both these answers point to significant qualities of the Renaissance spectacular stage, they do not really touch on the central issues: Why the intensity of interest in this mode of asserting the hierarchy? Why the enormous investment in this particular expression of magnificence? These are, at bottom, basic questions about the way in which the age saw itself.

Up to this point I have confined my discussion to drama; but, as we have seen, settings and machines were not used primarily for the production of plays. The new stage was developed largely for court masques, which were not, to the Renaissance, a kind of drama.

It is important to begin by insisting on the difference
between the two genres and by stressing the depth of
the age's commitment to the masque as a form of expression. Masques were essential to the life of the Renaissance court; their allegories gave a higher meaning
to the realities of politics and power, their fictions
created heroic roles for the leaders of society. Critics
from Puritan times onward have treated them as mere
extravagances, self-indulgent ephemera. But in the culture of the Medici grand dukes, the courts of Navarre,
Anjou, Valois, and Bourbon, the Venetian republic, the
Austrian archdukes, Henry VIII, extravagance in rulers
was not a vice but a virtue, an expression of magnanimity, and the idealizations of art had power and meaning. This was the context in which James I, and above
all Charles I, saw their own courts.

To the Renaissance, appearing in a masque was not
merely playing a part. It was, in a profound sense, precisely the opposite. When Inigo Jones and Ben Jonson
presented Queen Anne as Bel-Anna, Queen of the
Ocean, or King James as Pan, the universal god, or
Henry Prince of Wales as Oberon, Prince of Faery, a
deep truth about the monarchy was realized and embodied in action, and the monarchs were revealed in
roles that expressed the strongest Renaissance beliefs
about the nature of kingship, the obligations and per-
quisites of royalty. Masques were games and shows,
triumphs and celebrations; they were for the court and
about the court, and their seriousness was indistinguish-
able from their recreative quality. In England the form
had roots in a strong native tradition of mummings

and disguisings. It came into its own artistically with the accession of the first British Renaissance monarch, Henry VIII, who loved playing the central role in any enterprise, and retained the great composer William Cornysshe and the musicians of his Chapel Royal to provide his revels. For the next century and a half masques were staple elements of the Christmas and Shrovetide seasons, and formed an indispensable part of the courtly celebration of any extraordinary event, whether personal, social, or political—a royal marriage, the visit of a foreign dignitary, the conclusion of a treaty. In form they were infinitely variable, but certain characteristics were constant: the monarch was at the center, and they provided roles for members of the court within an idealized fiction. The climactic moment of the masque was nearly always the same: the fiction opened outward to include the whole court, as masquers descended from pageant car or stage and took partners from the audience. What the noble spectator watched he ultimately became.

The greatest problems in such a form are posed by protocol. Masquers are not actors; a lady or gentleman participating in a masque remains a lady or gentleman, and is not released from the obligation of observing all the complex rules of behavior at court. The king and queen dance in masques because dancing is the perquisite of every lady and gentleman. But playing a part, becoming an actor or actress, constitutes an impersonation, a lie, a denial of the true self. Hence "Woman-Actors," said William Prynne in 1633, with a large body of British opinion behind him, were "notorious whores."[1] For speaking roles, therefore, professionals had to be used, and this meant that the form, composite by nature, was in addition divided between players and masquers, actors and dancers. In the hands of Ben Jonson and Inigo Jones, this practical consideration became a metaphysical conceit, and the form as they developed it for James I and his queen, Anne of Denmark, rapidly separated into two sections. The first, called the antimasque, was performed by professionals, and presented a world of disorder or vice, everything that the ideal world of the second, the courtly main masque, was to overcome and supersede.

The masque presents the triumph of an aristocratic community; at its center is a belief in the hierarchy and a faith in the power of idealization. Philosophically, it is both Platonic and Machiavellian; Platonic because it presents images of the good to which the participants aspire and may ascend; Machiavellian because its idealizations are designed to justify the power they celebrate. As a genre, it is the opposite of satire; it educates by praising, by creating heroic roles for the leaders of society to fill. The democratic imagination sees only flattery in this sort of thing, but the charge is misguided, and blinds us to much that is crucial in all the arts of the Renaissance. The age believed in the *power* of art—to persuade, transform, preserve—and masques can no more be dismissed as flattery than portraits can. We do not consider portraits less "serious" than historical or religious or mythological paintings; nor do we assume that they have meaning only to their sitters; nor

[1] In *Histrio-Mastix, or the Scourge of Players,* 1633. See below, pp. 43-44.

do we believe them to be beneath the dignity of a Titian
or a Rubens.

It is probably the ephemeral quality of the form that
really disturbs us most, conditioned by a strongly moral
sense of artistic economy—all that money for only two
performances! In fact, this was a standard Puritan objection to the masque, though with an important difference: the Puritan objection did not distinguish the
masque from any other kind of art. Cromwell also
closed the theaters, sold off the royal picture collection,
and ordered statues defaced. We, however, do distinguish the arts; we assume that the ephemeral nature of
the masque calls into question not only its potential as
an investment, but even its seriousness. Behind this is
another moral assumption, generally unacknowledged:
that artists ought not to take such a form seriously; and
that if they say they are doing so, they are dissembling
their true motives. These claims are very common
among modern scholars, but a little historical perspective will allow us to dispose of them. Renaissance festi-
vals were the province of the greatest artists of the age;
their number included Leonardo, Dürer, Mantegna,
Holbein, Bronzino, Rubens, Buontalenti, Caron, Pri-
maticcio, Callot, Monteverdi, Ferrabosco, Dowland,
Campion, Lawes, Ronsard, Sidney, Jonson, and Milton.
Masques and triumphs regularly had enormously elaborate and complex philosophical and symbolic pro-
grammes; the idea that these were somehow inap-
propriate to the form is both historically inaccurate and
on the face of it illogical. No such charge appears until
well into the seventeenth century, at which time it is
rightly considered very new, and, as we shall see, both

subversive and revolutionary. The question of seriousness, however, does bring us back to the main issues. A
look at the exchequer records will show us that the
court was indubitably serious about masques, and believed that there' was some point in having the most
distinguished artists devise them. In what ways, then,
were masques serious?

Let us begin with the ways in which the age saw the
monarchy. The Renaissance had many concepts of
kingship, but central to all of them was the notion of
the ruler as an exemplary figure. This was true whether
he was conceived as God's regent on earth or as a
Machiavellian politician, and throughout all the grada-
tions in between. An Aristotelian might maintain that
to be a good king it is necessary to have all the virtues,
and a Machiavellian object that it is necessary only to
seem to have them; but in either case it is the *image* of
the monarch that is crucial, the appearance of virtue,
whether it accords with an inner reality or not. The
theatrical metaphor was a natural expression of such
an attitude: "We princes, I tell you," said Queen Elizabeth, "are set on stages, in the sight and view of all the
world duly observed." [2] James I made this a precept for
his heir in his handbook of kingship, *Basilikon Doron:*
"A King is as one set on a stage, whose smallest actions
and gestures, all the people gazingly doe behold." [3] The
monarch must not only impóse good laws, he must

[2] J. E. Neale, *Elizabeth I and her Parliaments* (New York,
1958) 2:119.
[3] C. H. McIlwain, ed., *Political Works of James I* (Cambridge, Mass., 1918), p. 43.

exemplify them "with his vertuous life in his owne person, and the person of his court and company; by good example alluring his subjects to the love of virtue, and hatred of vice. . . . Let your owne life be a law-booke and a mirrour to your people, that therein they may read the practise of their owne Lawes; and therein they may see, by your image, what life they should leade." [4]

Masques were the festal embodiments of this concept of monarchy. To Ben Jonson, far from being flattery, they were "the mirrors of man's life, whose ends, for the excellence of their exhibitors (as being the donatives of great princes to their people) ought always to carry a mixture of profit with them no less than delight." [5] Nor was the profit conceived in general or abstract terms. Court masques were always topical; under Charles I they argued the royal case in current political and legal disputes with an energy and ingenuity that suggests that the king must have been actively involved in their composition. Charles was not merely being entertained by his masques; the form was an extension of the royal mind, and—despite the universal British prejudice against actors—to take the stage was a royal prerogative. Perhaps the clearest illustration of how important the crown felt this prerogative to be may be found in the case of William Prynne, whose harsh words on women actors have already been cited.

Prynne was a barrister of Lincoln's Inn, an energetic and at times fanatical Puritan polemicist. In 1633 he pub-

[4] *Ibid.,* p. 30.
[5] *Love's Triumph through Callipolis,* lines 3 ff.

lished a gigantic attack on the theater entitled *Histrio-Mastix, or the Scourge of Players*. The books consists of a thousand pages of circular arguments and lunatic fulminations, but its authorities are the Bible and the church fathers, and it therefore carried weight with Puritan readers. The royal interest in drama is naturally, for Prynne, especially reprehensible. Watching plays is declared to be the "cause of untimely ends in Princes," and the histrionic Nero is adduced as an example. "Women-Actors, notorious whores" appears as an entry in the index; the king's attorney general took it to be an aspersion on the queen's participation in court theatricals. Prynne denied the allegation, but the evidence was considered ample, and he was arrested and charged, not with libel but with high treason. He was convicted by the Star Chamber and sentenced to life imprisonment, fined £5000, pilloried, expelled from Lincoln's Inn, deprived of his academic degree, and his ears were cut off by the public executioner.

Prynne was guilty not merely of an attack on the queen. There were many such that went unnoticed; against her Catholicism, her associates, her growing influence over the king. It was the attack on the queen as actress, on the royal theatricals, that was treasonable. The loss of Prynne's ears, freedom, and livelihood did not seem to the court too severe a penalty, nor did it seem to Prynne's Puritan supporters a punishment suffered in a trivial cause. Both sides rightly saw *The Scourge of Players* as a call to revolution, and Prynne became a popular hero.

Court masques and plays, then, were recognized to

be significant expressions of royal power. The most important Renaissance commentary on the subject is itself a theatrical one, Prospero's masque in *The Tempest*. It is, of course, not a real masque, but a dramatic representation of one, and it is unique in that its creator is also the monarch at its center. This is Shakespeare's essay on the power and art of the royal imagination. By 1611, when *The Tempest* was produced at Whitehall before the king, the playwright's knowledge of the work of Jones and Jonson must have been intimate. With James's accession in 1603 Shakespeare's company had come directly under the king's patronage; he and the other directors were made Grooms of the Chamber, members of the royal household, and wore the royal livery. We know that after 1612 the King's Men were the regular professional players employed in the Christmas masques, and it is reasonable to assume that they had been at least occasionally so employed from the beginning of the reign. That all this conferred a new status on the company of actors is attested by the fact that around 1612 they also began calling themselves not merely the King's Men or the King's Servants, but Gentlemen, the King's Servants. Shakespeare's figure of Prospero, the royal illusionist, derives from a profound understanding of court theater and the quintessentially courtly theatrical form of the masque. Masques are the expression of the monarch's will, the mirrors of his mind.

Prospero produces his masque to celebrate the betrothal of his daughter Miranda to Ferdinand, heir to the throne of Naples; it is both a royal masque and a

wedding masque. The lovers are shown a pastoral vision, presided over by Ceres and Juno. The goddess of
agriculture directs the play back to civilized nature,
away from Caliban's search for pig-nuts and the myster-
ious scammels, away from his dams for fish; and the
goddess of power takes on her most benign aspect as
patroness of marriage, pointing the way to a resolution
of political conflicts, to the proper exercise of authority
and the uniting of ancient enemies in nuptial harmony.
All the destructive elements of love have been banished.
Venus and Cupid, confounded by the chaste vows of
Ferdinand and Miranda, are safely elsewhere. The
agent of all this is Iris, the rainbow, the messenger of
heaven and the pledge of God's providence after the
universal flood.

The Tempest is temporally the most tightly and precisely organized of all Shakespeare's plays, the only
one in which the action represented takes precisely as
long as the performance of it. But the action of
Prospero's masque has a different time scheme; it
moves from "spongy April" through spring and high
summer to the entry of "certain reapers," "sunburnt
sicklemen, of August weary." After this Ceres promises
Ferdinand and Miranda not the coming of winter, but

> Spring come to you at the farthest,
> In the very end of harvest.

The masque's world is able to banish even winter. As
its love contains no lust, its natural cycle includes no
death. Appropriately, it is at this point that the magician interrupts his creation to recall himself and the

play to the other realities of the world of action. "I had forgot that foul conspiracy of the beast Caliban": it is precisely death, in the persons of Caliban, Stephano, and Trinculo, that threatens at this very moment. Prospero's awareness of time comprehends both masque and drama, both the seasonal cycle of endless fruition and the crisis of the dramatic moment. This awareness is both his art and his power, producing on the one hand his sense of his world as an insubstantial pageant, and on the other, his total command of the action moment by moment.

Prospero's vision of nature, then, is a vision in two senses. First, it is an imaginative projection for an audience—both the lovers and ourselves—of an ideal, a world of ordered and controlled nature from which all the dangerous potentialities have been banished. But it is also *Prospero's* vision, something unique to him, and a realization of the qualities of mind that have been controlling the play. The masque, with its apparitions and songs, and even more directly the tiny spectacular charades that Ariel performs for the shipwreck victims, are the royal magician's power conceived as art. In an obvious way that power is the power of imagination, but only if we take all the terms of the phrase literally. Imagination here is real power: to rule, to control and order the world, to change or subdue other men, to create; and the source of the power is imagination, the ability to make images, to project the workings of the mind outward in a physical, active form, to actualize ideas, to conceive actions.

The mind for Prospero, then, is an active and out-

going faculty (not, that is, a contemplative one), and
the relation between his art and his power is made very
clear by the play. His control over nature is exemplified
in the masque, performed by spirits, extensions of his
will, who act, in both senses, at his direction; Ariel, the
spirit of air, is his servant; the destructive elemental
forces are his to command. After the storm he has raised
at the play's opening, he lays aside his wand, the symbol
of his power, with the words "Lie there my art." [6]
Miranda describes his power in the same terms:

> If by your art, my dearest father, you have
> Put the wild waters in this roar, allay them;

and she continues,

> Had I been any god of power, I would
> Have sunk the sea within the earth. . . .[7]

Prospero is, of course, that god of power his daughter
wishes to be: it is primarily his authority over elemental
nature that is, for the age, godlike.

Modern critics are made exceedingly uncomfortable
by the idea of Prospero as God. Can Shakespeare have
meant to deify a figure so arbitrary, ill-tempered, vin-
dictive? But Renaissance Christianity was not a com-
forting faith; we find Milton's God equally unsympathetic, and for similar reasons. Even the gentle George
Herbert characterizes Christ in terms that are strikingly
reminiscent of Miranda's view of her father: "Storms
are the triumph of his art"; and a few lines later refers

[6] 1.2.25.   [7] 1.2.1–11.

to him explicitly as "the God of Power." [8] We want our God all love, our Jesus meek and mild, but Herbert's God is, like Prospero, a god of storms and power too.

As with gods in the Renaissance, so with kings. Here is the legal philosopher John Selden on the right of monarchs to bar their territorial waters to foreign shipping:

> For, seeing it is in the power of an Owner, so to use and enjoy his Own . . . , it cannot be amiss for any one to say, that the Seas, which might pass into the Dominion of any person, are by the Law of Dominion shut to all others who are not owners or that do not enjoy such a particular Right; in the same manner almost as that, whereby in that Winterseason they become unnavigable by the Law of Nature.[9]

Selden was not a fanatical supporter of Divine Right; on the contrary, he was a strong and litigious opponent of the autocracy of Charles I. Nevertheless he assumes that the appropriate analogy to the royal will in a commonwealth is the law of nature.

Again and again masques draw the same analogy. Pastoral, that traditionally contemplative mode, becomes an assertion of royal power; and the use of pastoral in masques is a remarkable index to the age's changing attitudes toward the monarchy. We may trace in this a significant development. In the early years of James I, when a pastoral scene appears as part of a sequence, contrasted with cities or palaces, it invariably comes at the beginning and embodies the wildness of nature or the untutored innocence that we pass

[8] "The Bag," lines 5, 9.
[9] *Mare Clausum* (London, 1663), f2r.

beyond to clear visions of sophistication and order, usually represented by complex machines and Palladian architecture. But after about a decade, from 1616 onward, this sequence is reversed. When pastoral settings appear they come at the end, and embody the ultimate ideal that the masque asserts. For the earlier sequence we might take as the normative masque Jonson's *Oberon,* which opens with "a dark rock with trees beyond it and all wildness that could be presented," then moves to a rusticated castle, and concludes with a Palladian interior. For the later sequence, a good example is Jonson's *Vision of Delight,* which opens with a perspective of fair buildings, changes to mist and cloud, and concludes with the Bower of the Spring. There are of course any number of other instances, but the important point is that the sequences are invariable: in a Stuart court masque with this sort of structure, when a pastoral scene appears before 1616 it always comes at the beginning, after 1616 it always comes at the end.

Obviously two different notions of both nature and the function of pastoral are at work here. But the change is really more interesting for what it says about the masque and its patrons than for what it says about pastoral—it is no news that to the Renaissance, nature was either better or worse than civilization. There is more than mere contrast in Jones's and Jonson's transitions. In the early productions they conceive the masque as starting somewhere else, very far from the realities of Whitehall: a landscape, a great red cliff, an ugly hell. But the work concludes with the realities of the court: the queen on a throne surrounded by her ladies, or in a classical House of Fame; the Prince of Wales emerging from a Palladian *tempietto*. The architecture of these final visions extends the architecture of the colonnaded and galleried Banqueting House in which the performance itself is taking place, just as spectator merges with masquer in the great central dance.

But the later productions tend to start with the realities of Whitehall—in the cellars, in the court buttery hatch, or most often simply in the masquing hall itself, and the masque begins by claiming that what is taking place is not fiction but reality. Indeed, in the most extraordinary example, Jones, ignoring Jonson's text (which demands an indoor scene) opens *Time Vindicated* (1623) with a perspective setting of the façade of his own uncompleted Banqueting House. Even this, London's new Palladian masterpiece, is rejected in favor of a final pastoral vision of Diana and Hippolytus in a wood. The Caroline productions go even further, and tend to resolve all action through pastoral transformations. The apotheoses of nature become immensely complex and inclusive visual statements about the commonwealth, accommodating within their vistas even traditionally anti-pastoral elements—distant views of London, the fleet in full sail, the fortified castle at Windsor.

What is recorded in these productions is the growth of a political ideology. The masques of James I and Charles I express the developing movement toward autocracy—it is not accidental that Jones's pastoral visions become most elaborate during the 1630s, the decade of prerogative rule. Monarchs like Charles and his queen are doubtless attracted to the vision of themselves as pastoral deities because the metaphor expresses only the most benign aspects of absolute monarchy. If we can really see the king as the tamer of nature, the queen as the goddess of flowers, there will be no problems about Puritans or Ireland or Ship Money. Thus the ruler gradually redefines himself through the illusionist's art, from a hero, the center of a court and a culture, to the god of power, the center of a universe. Annually he transforms winter to spring, renders the savage wilderness benign, makes earth fruitful, restores the golden age. We tend to see in such productions only elegant compliments offered to the monarch. In fact they are offered not to him but by him, and they are direct political assertions.

We might compare John Selden on the king's will as the law of nature with Jonson's justification of the appearance of spring in midwinter in *The Vision of Delight* (1617). The dialogue is between Fantasy and Wonder, embodiments of the creativity of the artist and the response of the spectator. Wonder asks,

> Whence is it that the air so sudden clears,
> And all things in a moment turn so mild?
> Whose breath or beams have got proud Earth with child
> Of all the treasure that great Nature's worth,
> And makes her every minute to bring forth?
> How comes it winter is so quite forced hence,
> And locked up underground? . . .
> Whose power is this? What god?

Fantasy replies, gesturing toward King James,

> Behold a king
> Whose presence maketh this perpetual spring,

> The glories of which spring grow in that bower,
> And are the marks and beauties of his power.[10]

What is expressed through the unseasonable glories of nature and the scenic marvels of Vitruvian mechanics is royal power. The choir takes up the theme, turning it to a political affirmation, and initiating the court's revels:

> 'Tis he, 'tis he, and no power else
> That makes all this what Fant'sy tells;
> The founts, the flowers, the birds, the bees,
> The herds, the flocks, the grass, the trees
> Do all confess him; but most these
> Who call him lord of the four seas,
> King of the less and greater isles,
> And all these happy when he smiles.
> > Advance, his favor calls you to advance,
> > And do your this night's homage in a dance.[11]

The culmination of pastoral is, in the masque, the state and the court.

Or again, Jonson's *Mercury Vindicated from the Alchemists at Court.* The masque opens with alchemists practising below stairs; they have enslaved Mercury in their search for the Philosophers' Stone. They succeed, however, in producing only the deformed creatures who dance the antimasque. A seventeenth-century spectator would have seen more than contrast in the subsequent transition to the Bower of Nature: Mercury is the patron of alchemy precisely because he is the active principle in nature, and the concluding vision places him in his proper context. The metamorphosis is ef-

[10] Lines 164–192.   [11] Lines 194–203.

fected by the god himself invoking the present majesty, King James: "Vanish with thy insolence, thou and thy imposters, and all mention of you melt before the majesty of this light, whose Mercury I profess to be, and never more the philosophers' ".[12] At this the alchemists' workshop vanished, and "the whole scene changed to a glorious bower wherein Nature was placed with Prometheus at her feet." Prometheus signified to the Renaissance human potentiality. As Mercury is freed, so Nature is restored by the royal power: "How young and fresh I feel tonight," she sings. The masque concludes, through its pastoral vision, with a living emblem of man's creativity.

Jonson's final masque, the pastoral *Chloridia,* with Queen Henrietta Maria at its center, and addressed to King Charles, abandons entirely the passive and contemplative aspects of the form, and becomes a hymn to the life of action. It manages to include among its various nymphs, floods, rivers, fountains, flowers, the very uncharacteristic figure of Fame, that arch-enemy of pastoral contentment, that last mental infirmity, that source of laborious days. She is accompanied by personifications of Poetry, traditional enough in pastoral, but also by History, and the city arts of Architecture and Sculpture, all uniting to sing the praises of the Caroline monarchy.

The vision of nature controlled by the human intellect is a central way of expressing the sovereign's place in the Renaissance universe. This is why the ceilings of palaces are so often, like the Whitehall Banqueting

[12] Lines 166 ff.

House, decorated with paintings depicting the apotheosis of the monarchy within a benign heaven. We put
roofs on our houses because without them we are at the
mercy of the weather. But having done so, the Renaissance ruler went on to create an alternative heaven,
asserting his control over his environment and the divinity of his rule through the power of the art at his command. All this is a fantasy, no doubt; but it is a fantasy
not only of monarchists and their artists. It is the chief
end of Baconian science as well. "Of the sciences which
regard nature," wrote Bacon in *The Great Instauration,*
"it is the glory of God to conceal a thing, but it is the
glory of the King to find a thing out." [13] The glory of
the *king,* not of the scientist. The Renaissance empir-
icist was able to list among the promised benefits of the
new learning the most fabulous wonders of masques:
dominion over the seasons, the raising of storms at will,
the acceleration of germination and harvest.[14] Every
masque is a celebration of this concept of science, a
ritual in which the society affirms its wisdom and asserts its control over its world and its destiny.

For modern readers, the scientific assumptions of the
masque and the stage that was created for it require
particular emphasis, because we are much more likely
to view the form in terms of magic than of science.
Thus a recent and very influential critic writes that the
elaborate mechanics of the masque "were being used,
partially at least, for magical ends, to form a vast mov-

[13] R. F. Jones, ed., *Essays, etc.* (New York, 1937), p. 251.
[14] *Magnalia Naturae,* in Bacon's *Works,* edd. Ellis, Spedding,
and Heath (London, 1887–1892) 3:167–168.

ing and changing talisman which should call down divine powers to the assistance of the monarch." [15] Possibly; but no contemporary observer ever writes about the form in this way, and when the creators of masques explain what they are doing, it has nothing to do with magic. It has to do with wit and understanding, with the ability to control natural forces through intellect, with comprehending the laws of nature, and most of all, with our own virtue and self-knowledge. There are, to be sure, ways of describing virtue, knowledge, and science as magic, but that is not how the masques describe them. And when magic appears in the masques, it is regularly counteracted not by an alternative sorcery, black magic defeated by white magic, but by the clear voice of reason, constancy, heroism. Inigo Jones wrote that he had devised his splendid costume for Queen Henrietta Maria in *Tempe Restored* "so that corporeal beauty, consisting in symmetry, color, and certain unexpressible graces, shining in the queen's majesty, may draw us to the contemplation of the beauty of the soul, unto which it hath analogy." [16] Masques are not magical talismans, they are analogies, ideals made apprehensible, so that we may know ourselves and see what we may become.

This is not to say that such a patron as Charles I did not rely on these visions of permanence and transcendence in a way that we may call magical. There are always people who believe in magic. He also relied on judicial decisions, architectural façades, and depictions

[15] Frances Yates, *Theatre of the World* (London, 1969) p. 86.
[16] Lines 361–364.

of himself in imperial trappings in precisely the same way, and, like all magical thinkers, without any ability to perceive such phenomena in relation to their real effects. But insofar as the texts give us evidence, Jones and his poets did not think of their creations in this way. What is provided for the court is not a mystic charm, but roles to play that relate the present to the heroic ideals of the past on the one hand, and to the immutable laws of nature on the other. They teach, they celebrate virtue, they persuade by example; they lead the court to its ideal self through wonder.

So the king is allegorized in ways that imply intellect, control, power: as Neptune, tamer of the elements, or Pan, the god of nature, or the life-giving sun, or, in a Jonsonian *tour de force,* as pure energy, a principle of physics, through whom the ultimate mysteries of infinite power and perpetual motion are finally solved:

> Not that we think you weary be,
> For he
> That did this motion give,
> And made it so long live,
> Could likewise give it perpetuity.
> Nor that we doubt you have not more,
> And store
> Of changes to delight;
> For they are infinite,
> As is the power that brought those forth before.[17]

Jonson's metaphor expresses not only the absolute authority increasingly asserted by the Stuart monarchy, but even more the age's wonder at the infinite possibil-

---

[17] *News from the New World,* lines 342–351.

ities of machinery scenic or otherwise. The metaphor
will seem less far-fetched if we set beside it a passage
by Marsilio Ficino, the great Florentine neo-Platonist,
discussing mechanical models of the heavenly spheres:

> Since man has observed the order of the heavens, when they
> move, whither they proceed and with what measures, and
> what they produce, who could deny that man possesses as
> it were almost the same genius as the Author of the heavens?
> And who could deny that man could also make the heavens,
> could he only obtain the instruments and the heavenly ma-
> terial, since even now he makes them, though of a different
> material, but still with a very similar order? [18]

This is the context within which the court audience
saw the masque, with its scenic illusions and spectacular
machines: as models of the universe, as science, as assertions of power, as demonstrations of the essential divinity of the human mind. The marvels of stagecraft—the
ability to overcome gravity, control the natural world,
reveal the operation of the heavenly spheres—are the
supreme expressions of Renaissance kingship.

[18] From *Platonic Theology,* trans. Josephine L. Burroughs,
Journal of the History of Ideas 5 (April, 1944):235.

3

The Role of King

Hostile critics saw in the royal histrionics only frivolity or hypocrisy, and even sympathic observers regularly referred to masques as "vanities." This, indeed, is Prospero's term for his own masque, "some vanity of mine art." [1] The description is exact and the charge irrefutable: these works are totally self-regarding. They are designed to be so. "All representations," wrote Ben Jonson, "especially those of this nature in court, public spectacles, either have been or ought to be the mirrors of man's life." [2] But mirrors, like so many Renaissance symbols, may be viewed in various and contradictory ways, and their moral implications lie in the eye of the beholder. They are emblems of worldliness and pride, frail glasses "which are as easy broke as they make forms." [3] They are also the way to self-knowledge. English didacticism in 1559 could do no better than provide a mirror for magistrates; and Hamlet's player

[1] *The Tempest* 4.1.41.
[2] *Love's Triumph through Callipolis,* lines 1–3.
[3] *Measure for Measure* 2.4.123–26.

holding the mirror up to nature is not encouraging her self-esteem. For the Jacobean translator of Ovid, the myth of Narcissus embodied the full ambiguity of the power of reflection. The youth's mother, reports George Sandys, *"enquiring whether he should live untill he were old,* Tiresias *replied:* If he know not himselfe. *As strange as obscure; and seeming contradictory to that Oracle of* Apollo: To know a mans selfe is the chiefest knowledge. *The lacke hereof hath ruined many: but having it must needs ruine our beautifull* Narcissus: *who only is in love with his owne perfections."* [4] This is a paradigm for the Stuart court and the mirror of its theater.

Roles in plays, to Puritan observers, were impostures and lies. The very act of imitation, in drama as in art, usurped a divine prerogative, and theatrical productions were therefore often seen to be at the heart of the court's degeneracy and impiety. But from another point of view the parts we choose to play are not impersonations but ideals. They are what we wish to be, and they reveal not so much the way we want others to see us as the way we want to see ourselves.

Here are some ways in which the Stuart court wanted to see itself.

The Masque of Queens

In 1609 Ben Jonson and Inigo Jones created a heroic masque for Queen Anne and her ladies. *The Masque*

[4] *Ovid's Metamorphoses Englished* (Oxford, 1632), p. 103.

of Queens provided a martial context for womanly virtue—whereas King James, we will recall, was an ardent and programmatic pacifist. The production opened on a coven of witches and an ugly hell; infernal dances and charms provided an elaborate and extended antimasque. Suddenly the hall was filled with a blast of loud music, "with which not only the hags themselves but the hell into which they ran quite vanished, and the whole face of the scene altered, scarce suffering the memory of such a thing. But in the place of it appeared a glorious and magnificent building figuring the House of Fame, in the top of which were discovered the twelve masquers sitting upon a throne triumphal erected in form of a pyramid and circled with all store of light."

Eleven of the masquers had the roles of warrior queens from history. In Jones's costume designs, the Amazonian qualities are expressed through a variety of details: an elegant bodice adapted from armor, a plumed helmet, masculine half-sleeves, bases, and instead of dancing pumps, light boots (Figure 8). For the twelfth queen, Anne of Denmark, Jonson invented the figure of Bel-Anna, Queen of the Ocean. Only the design for her headdress has survived (Figure 9). Jones has crowned her with an armillary sphere, a celestial globe. Just such a model as this had demonstrated to Ficino the power of human knowledge and the essential divinity of the mind.

Jones's drawing of the House of Fame is the earliest surviving design for stage machinery in England (Figure 10). The drawing shows the front of a hexagonal

FIGURE 8. The Masque of Queens: *costume for the Countess of Bedford as Penthesileia, Queen of the Amazons.*

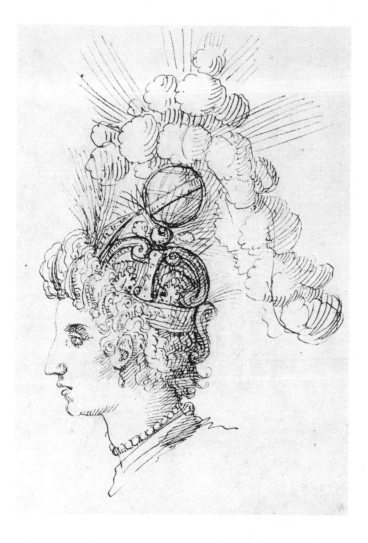

FIGURE 9. The Masque of Queens: *headdress for Anne of Denmark as Bel-Anna, Queen of the Ocean.*

FIGURE 10. The Masque of Queens: *scene 2, the House of Fame.*

building; it has double doors within a huge central arch, above which sit the twelve masquers on their pyramidal throne. The figures on the roof are probably musicians; the two deities in the clouds on either side of the cornice are identified by Jonson as "eminent figures of Honor and Virtue." The façade is adorned with statues. Those on the lower tier represent "the most excellent poets, as Homer, Virgil, Lucan, etc., as being the substantial supporters of Fame," while those on the upper are "Achilles, Aeneas, Caesar, and those great heroes which these poets had celebrated." The conception, Jonson says, derives from Chaucer.

The architecture of the building is a characteristic amalgam of styles. It has certain Palladian elements—the central arch, the pilasters, the windows of the lower story—but the basic motif of the upper tier is the gothic trefoil. In the same way, the statuary on the façade pays homage to classical heroes, but the house itself is a realization of the work of the greatest English medieval poet. The union of classic and romantic, heroic and chivalric, was a continual ideal of James's reign, and Jones's setting is an architectural assertion of the success of the synthesis. But Jonson also makes it clear that in the House of Fame, heroism is a secondary virtue: the heroes are glorified not by their deeds alone, but by the enduring and transforming power of poetry. Every hero has his poet, and the building is inspired by Chaucer. The whole vision presents the Jacobean court with its own best image. Heroism is the royal consort; but the highest virtue is that of the pacific king, not a warrior, but a classical scholar and poet.

This was the setting for the entry of the masquers. The pyramidal throne suddenly turned around, and in its place the winged figure of Fame appeared. The great gates then opened, and the ladies were borne forth into the hall in three triumphant chariots, drawn respectively by "far-sighted eagles, to note Fame's sharp eye," griffins, "that design / Swiftness and strength," and, for the queen's carriage, lions, "that imply / The top of graces, state and majesty."

Oberon

Like his mother, Henry Prince of Wales was an ardent masquer, and like his father, an antiquarian and patron of the arts. For the two seasons following *The Masque of Queens,* 1610 and 1611, he commissioned from Jonson and Jones two entertainments designed to restore to life the world of ancient British chivalry. For the first, *Prince Henry's Barriers,* he chose a role from the Arthurian romances, Meliadus, lover of The Lady of the Lake. In Jonson's fiction, the young prince is summoned by Merlin and King Arthur to revitalize English knighthood—the production centered about feats of arms in which Henry distinguished himself. A contemporary spectator records that "the Prince performed this challenge with wondrous skill and courage, to the great joy and admiration of all the beholders, the Prince not being full sixteene yeeres of age." [5]

[5] Stephen Orgel and Roy Strong, *Inigo Jones* (Berkeley, 1973), 1:159.

But the martial side of the prince's nature apparently disturbed King James, who vetoed a similar project for the next year. In honor of Henry's creation as Prince of Wales, Jonson and Jones devised instead the masque of *Oberon, The Fairy Prince*. Spenserian romance joins with classical myth to create a Britain that unites the traditions of chivalry with classical order. Silenus and his satyrs celebrate the accession of Oberon, heir of King Arthur—Greek and British mythology are, for Jonson, part of a single tradition. Indeed, in a gloss Jonson even suggests that the English word "fairy" is cognate with the Greek *féras,* a late form of *théras,* satyrs. The synthesis is again apparent in Jones's costume for the young prince (Figure 11). King James's heir is a medieval knight and Roman emperor combined; he also wears recognizable elements of contemporary dress. The Roman skirt, for example, has been transformed into Jacobean trunk hose. Oberon is not an impersonation, but a version of the true prince.

The palace Jones designed for Oberon is another synthesis, an anthology of architectural styles (Figure 12). A rusticated basement seems to grow out of the rocks. The parterre has a Palladian balustrade. A splendid pedimented archway fills the central façade, supported by grotesque Italian terms, and accented by Doric pilasters and Serlian windows. Crenellated English medieval turrets are topped with tiny baroque minarets; two pure Elizabethan chimneys frame an elegant dome in the style of Bramante.

Jones's inspiration here is not merely eclectic. Rather this design makes a programmatic visual statement

FIGURE 11. Oberon: *costume for Henry, Prince of Wales, as Oberon.*

FIGURE 12. Oberon: *scene 2, Oberon's palace*.

about the national culture and the sources of its heroism. England becomes great through the imposition of classical order upon British nature; the rough native strength of the castle is remade according to the best models, civilized by the arts of design, by learning and taste. In the same way the Prince of Faery, the new Prince of Wales, comes out of the woods, tames the rough satyrs, and descends to salute his father, the real King James, in the Palladian architecture of the Whitehall Banqueting House.

Such productions reveal a great deal about the age's sense of itself and its intense hopes for this young man. The king, for all his pacific policies (which in any case were not especially popular) was awkward and largely without charm. Henry's untimely death in 1612 robbed England not only of a patron for her poets and artists, but of a romantic hero as well.

Neptune's Triumph for the Return of Albion

In 1623 Prince Charles, the Duke of Buckingham, the prince's private secretary Sir Francis Cottington, and an odd assortment of others including the court dwarf Archibald Armstrong, went to Spain to negotiate the prince's marriage with the Infanta Maria, sister of Philip IV. The Spanish match was a favorite project of King James; it represented a major European alliance, and seemed to promise an eventual reconciliation with the Catholic faith and the powers that adhered to it. But it also involved large concessions to

the Catholic cause in England, and was therefore un-
derstandably unpopular with the British public. The
prince and his negotiators were eager for an agreement,
and undertook to meet all conditions; but the Spanish
court rightly felt that Charles's promises regarding the
necessary changes in the English laws of religious conformity were unrealistic, and after almost a year of discussions the plan was abandoned. The prince's party
sourly returned home in October 1624, to find their
failure greeted with popular rejoicing. To the king,
however, the whole episode must have seemed a galling
fiasco, and the court provided no celebrations of its
own.

Three months later Jonson and Jones prepared a
long delayed welcome home. *Neptune's Triumph for
the Return of Albion* does more than put the best face
on a bad situation. It provides a context within which
the fiasco may be seen as a victory. Jonson's fiction begins, like so many of his later masques, as fact: it opens
in the Banqueting House itself. The stage presents nothing but two pillars dedicated to Neptune; the masque
has not yet begun. A poet enters, ostensibly to distribute
playbills; the court cook appears, and requests an account of the forthcoming entertainment. The poet ex-
pounds his allegory:

> The mighty Neptune, mighty in his styles,
> And large command of waters and of isles,
> Not as the lord and sovereign of the seas,
> But chief in the art of riding, late did please
> To send his Albion forth . . .
> Through Celtiberia; and to assist his course,

Gave him his powerful Manager of Horse,
With divine Proteus, father of disguise,
To wait upon them with his counsels wise
In all extremes. His great commands being done,
And he desirous to review his son,
He doth dispatch a floating isle from hence
Unto the Hesperian shores to waft him thence.

In this allegory, King James is Neptune, Prince Charles Albion; Buckingham is visible under his title of Master of the King's Horse in the first of Albion's associates; and Cottington, who had served as a secret agent, is Proteus. The journey is "through Celtiberia" because their route took them first to Paris, but the reason for the expedition is carefully glossed over. The floating island is then described. The royal party will make its appearance enthroned beneath a mystical Tree of Harmony, the banyan, first planted in India by the sun himself. The tree becomes a symbol of the harmonious strength of the court; every one of its branches sends out roots, and becomes a new trunk supporting the whole.

The cook demands more entertainment, the comedy of an antimasque. The poet replies that his work is high art, addressed only to the intellect. But the cook then articulates Jonson's own concept of theater at court: these presentations speak to the whole man, and must satisfy all his senses; they are given in the Banqueting House because they are not merely poems but banquets, ravishing sights and sounds, sweet smells; they feed all parts of the observer's sensibility. And the cook himself then produces the comic dancers, in the form of meats and vegetables from his own gigantic cooking pot.

Now the poet's masque begins. The heavens open revealing Apollo and Mercury (patrons respectively of the poetry of the masque and the prose of the anti-masque), accompanied by the muses and the goddess Harmony. To their music the floating island appears, and moves forward bearing the masquers (Figure 13). Jones's island is covered with an arbor, as the text requires; but it is an arbor of palms, not a banyan tree. In part, this doubtless reflects merely the architect's ignorance of Asian botany; however the choice of palms can hardly have been accidental. The all-powerful Neptune's island bears emblems of peace; the returning prince appears beneath the branches that heralded Christ's entry into Jerusalem.

The association of James's pacifism with the peace of God, and of his capital with the holy city, formed an important part of Jacobean official imagery from the very beginning of the reign, and as a way of justifying unpopular policies, particularly in ecclesiastical matters, it became increasingly insistent. James was regularly represented as Solomon (for example, he is so depicted by Rubens on the Banqueting House ceiling), and the Anglican church under the Stuart monarchy was held to preserve the pristine purity of Christ and the Apostles. The line of argument ran this way: England was converted by Joseph of Arimathea, long before Constantine and the conversion of Rome. The decay of Christianity began with the advent of Augustine and his popish monks, but the abolition of the English

FIGURE 13. Neptune's Triumph: *the floating island of Macaria.*

monasteries had allowed the ancient faith to flower again. All of this is implied in Jones's emblematic palms.

But the masque makes a more overt set of claims for the monarchy as well. James is explicitly represented, after all, not as Solomon but as Neptune. With the descent of the masquers the island disappears, and Jones's scene opens to reveal a marine palace (Figure 14). James's Palladian Banqueting House is now translated into the deep perspective of a maritime fantasy. Behind the allegorization of the king as Neptune lies a long tradition. In the same way, Sir Walter Ralegh had sung the Ocean's love to Cynthia, the moon, ruler of the sea; and Jonson and Jones in 1609 had presented Queen Anne not as the sovereign of the realm but as Bel-Anna, Queen of the Ocean. There is, of course, a simple military reality behind this: the strength of an island kingdom depends heavily on its navy. But there are mythographic realities as well that tell us a good deal more about the way the Stuart court saw itself. Neptune appears in the masque "Not as the lord and sovereign of the seas"—he is that in any case—"But chief in the art of riding."

The connection between these two aspects of the royal persona would not have seemed obscure to a Jacobean audience who knew that King James's favorite sport was riding. But Jonson's allusion goes deeper, to a myth in which Neptune was the creator and tamer of the embodiment of the ocean's energy, the horse. From Plato onward, horsemanship had served as a symbol for the imposition of reason upon the wildness of nature or the violence of the passions. This is why

FIGURE 14. Neptune's Triumph: *the palace of Oce-anus.*

the implications of the term chivalry are so much more complex than its derivation—from *chevalerie,* horsemanship—would suggest. To bring the destructive energies of nature under control, both within and without, was the end of Renaissance education and science. Every gentleman was thus properly a type of Neptune; and on a larger scale, the myth provided a pattern for the relation between king and commonwealth.

That the pattern was unrealistic goes without saying. The only mind operating in Jonson's allegory is the monarch's. Albion's return is a triumph because it is executed at Neptune's command; the whole action is presented as a serene extension of the royal will. This is a political myth, an accurate record of the way James viewed his government in his last years. His son's autocracy is only a step beyond. But the danger of political myths lies in their tendency to exclude political realities: the mirror of the king's mind allows him to know only himself. By 1624 the commonwealth, unlike the sea or the horse, had developed a very strong mind of its own. And indeed, in this penultimate year of his reign, political realities denied the king even his theatrical triumph. The French and Spanish ambassadors could not be invited to attend together, and each threatened the most dire diplomatic reprisals if the other were given priority. Within two days of the performance, James was forced to cancel the masque.

The Triumph of Peace and *Coelum Britannicum*

The development of Charles I's autocracy is one of the most extraordinary chapters in British legal history.

In 1629, outraged by what he took to be continual in-
roads on the crown's authority, frustrated by inadequate
revenues and the failure of numerous proposals for new
taxes, the king dissolved Parliament and determined to
rule without it. He managed to do so for the next
eleven years. The 1630s saw the most complete consoli-
dation of royal power in British history; by 1635 the
king claimed the rights of direct taxation, the granting
of monopolies in all industries, the control of all ecclesiastical offices including those in private households,
the enforcement of absolute religious conformity—
even the manufacture of soap was declared to be a royal
prerogative. No area of the nation's life was too insignificant for Charles to want to regulate it: for example, by royal edict alehouses were forbidden to sell
tobacco, and London inns to serve game. (The latter
measure was conceived as a way of making town life so
unpleasant for country gentlemen that they would be
persuaded to return home to manage their estates.)

There were many challenges to the legality of the
royal prerogatives. In every case, the basic question was
whether laws could be made by royal fiat, without the
assent of parliament. Gradually over the decade, usually
by the barest possible majority, the courts came to support the king. By 1638, when the Star Chamber handed
down its decision in the famous ship-money case [6] that

---

[6] The king had revived an Elizabethan tax on coastal towns
for the support of the navy. In 1633 the tax was extended to
inland districts, and met with considerable resistance, the op-
ponents arguing that the imposition of ship-money constituted
taxation by royal fiat. The test case was Rex v. Hampden, 1637;
the decision was overturned by Parliament in 1641.

rex was *lex,* that king was law, the British monarchy
was *statutorily* the most powerful in Europe. The political realities were, of course, quite different. Only
authority can derive from statute. A government's
power depends on its ability to enforce its authority.
The crown might impose taxes, but people increasingly
refused to pay them; and if they could not be persuaded
to do so by noble rhetoric and high ideals, the king's
only recourse was an army that had to be paid out of
uncollected taxes. Such realities produced in Charles
only patient bafflement at the stubborn unregeneracy of
so ungrateful a populace; he ruled according to a political theory that had the quality of a hermetic allegory. In a very profound way the stage at Whitehall
was his truest kingdom, the masque the most accurate
expression of his mind.

The legal profession was on the whole uncomfortable about royal prerogatives, and unsympathetic to the
crucial principle of Divine Right, which made the king
responsible only to God. In 1634 the Inns of Court took
the remarkable step of retaining Inigo Jones and James
Shirley in an attempt to speak to the king in his own
language. The lawyers presented a masque at Whitehall that was, for all its courtly splendor, diplomatically
but unequivocally critical of the royal policies, and undertook, through the power of poetry and the marvels
of spectacle, to persuade the royal spectator to return to
the rule of law.

The impulse to produce *The Triumph of Peace* came,
oddly enough, from a royal command. William Prynne,
author of *Histrio-Mastrix,* with its treasonable attack

on court theatricals, had been indicted, and his trial
was about to begin. The prisoner was a barrister of
Lincoln's Inn, and had dedicated the offending volume
to his fellow lawyers. Charles demanded that the legal
fraternities definitively repudiate their colleague and
publicly declare their loyalty to the crown. What gesture of loyalty could be more appropriate than the pre-
sentation of a lawyers' masque at court?

The Inns lavishly complied. Shirley composed his
text in consultation with a committee of barristers; the
subject of *The Triumph of Peace* was the relationship
between the king and the law. The setting Jones provided for the masque's opening was an Italian piazza
(Figure 15). In fact, Shirley had given the architect a
choice; the text calls for a scene "representing the
Forum or Piazza of Peace." Jones chose not a classical
Roman forum, but the center of the life of an Italian
Renaissance city-state, the architectural embodiment of
republican principles. In contrast, two years earlier
when Jones created a similar setting for the king's
masque *Albion's Triumph,* the architecture had been
a clear expression of imperial ideals (Figure 16).

The Roman analogy is carefully avoided in *The Triumph of Peace.* Extravagantly and with unparallelled
splendor the legal profession asserted to the crown their
joint responsibilities:

> The world shall give prerogative to neither;
> We cannot flourish but together.

Not surprisingly, considering the nature of the medium,
the message failed to get across. The masque was a

FIGURE 15. The Triumph of Peace: *scene 1, the Piazza of Peace*.

FIGURE 16. Albion's Triumph: *the forum of Albipolis.*

huge success; the royal solipsist saw in it nothing but adulation, and was graciously pleased to order it repeated.[7]

Two weeks later the king presented his own view of his place in the commonwealth. Thomas Carew's and Inigo Jones's *Coelum Britannicum* was the greatest theatrical expression of the Caroline autocracy. Carew's allegory is about the radical reformation of society, the purifying of the mind and passions, the power of language and apparitions to exorcise the rebellious spirit; it even undertakes to create a new body of poetic symbolism, as if to redeem through its imagery the imperfect nature that art imitates. The masque conceives the royal will as central to an unprecedented degree. In its fable, Jove has taken the Caroline court as a model for his own, and has banished licentiousness and ignoble passion from the heavens. The opening scene is a ruined city, the decadent civilization that is to be revitalized and ennobled. Its shutters part, and the gigantic figure of Atlas fills the stage (Figure 17). For the Renaissance, Atlas was the exemplar of cosmic wisdom. Jones's heroic figure, crowned and bearing the heavens on his shoulders, is the link between earth and heaven, an allegory of the monarch described in *Basilikon Doron*. The great globe opens, revealing the constellations, those glorifications of ancient lust and violence, the mythology of an outworn past. Each in its turn is deposed and extinguished, until heaven at last

[7] For a detailed discussion of the masque's complex political context, and a full analysis of the allegory, see *Inigo Jones* 1:63–66.

FIGURE 17. Coelum Britannicum: *Atlas*.

stands empty, ready to receive a chaste and heroic iconography.

The reformation then begins. Atlas and the sphere vanish and a mountainous landscape appears (Figure 18). From beneath the stage come ancient Britons, the kingdom's history restored to life. (They are the figures shown seated on the rocks.) Above, wild nature is framed by the palms of the royal peace. This setting is to open, revealing first a garden and a princely villa, and then an elegant pastoral perspective with Windsor Castle in the distance, while the heavens will part to show beneficent deities smiling on Charles's reign.

The grandiloquence of the masque's conception lay as much in its engineering as in its poetry. Carew's text gives a vivid sense of the spectator's experience:

> . . . there began to rise out of the earth the top of a hill, which by little and little grew to be a huge mountain that covered all the scene; the underpart of this was wild and craggy, and above somewhat more pleasant and flourishing; about the middle part of this mountain were seated the three kingdoms of England, Scotland and Ireland, all richly attired in regal habits appropriated to the several nations, with crowns on their heads, and each of them bearing the ancient arms of the kingdoms they represented. At a distance above these sat a young man in a white embroidered robe, upon his fair hair an olive garland, with wings at his shoulders, and holding in his hand a cornucopia filled with corn and fruits, representing the genius of these kingdoms. . . .
>
> At this the underpart of the rock opens, and out of a cave are seen to come the masquers, richly attired like ancient heroes; the colours yellow embroidered with silver, their antique helms curiously wrought, and great plumes on the top; before them a troop of young lords and noblemen's

FIGURE 18. Coelum Britannicum: *proscenium and mountain scene.*

sons bearing torches of virgin wax; these were apparelled after the old British fashion in white coats embroidered with silver, girt, and full gathered, cut square-collared, and round caps on their heads, with a white feather wreathen about them; first these dance with their lights in their hands, after which the masquers descend into the room and dance their entry.

The dance being past, there appears in the further part of the heaven coming down a pleasant cloud, bright and transparent, which coming softly downwards before the upper part of the mountain, embraceth the genius, but so as through it all his body is seen; and then rising again with a gentle motion bears up the genius of the three kingdoms, and being past the airy region, pierceth the heavens, and is no more seen. At that instant the rock with the three king-doms on it sinks and is hidden in the earth. This strange spectacle gave great cause of admiration, but especially how so huge a machine, and of that great height, could come from under the stage, which was but six foot high.

The full force of Caroline idealism, the determina-tion to purify, reorder, reform, reconceive a whole cul-ture, is here fully realized in apparitions and marvelous machinery. The most complete expression of the royal will in the age lay not in the promulgation of edicts, erratically obeyed, nor in military power, inadequately furnished, but in Inigo Jones's ability to do the impos-sible.

Epilogue

Or rather, to seem to do so: the truth of the royal productions was the truth of appearances. Power was asserted only through analogies, faith affirmed only
through symbols. That such forms of expression should
now seem to us at best obscure, at worst insincere, says
much for the success of the Puritan revolution. History
has vindicated William Prynne; however extravagant
its rhetoric, the Puritan invective against royal theatricals reveals, ironically, an accurate sense of their
most powerful effects. Viewed from outside the Banqueting House, the masque could be seen to provide the
monarchy chiefly with an impenetrable insulation
against the attitudes of the governed. Year after year
designer and poet recreated an ideal commonwealth, all
its forces under rational control, its people uniquely
happy and endlessly grateful.

It is a mistake to think that there was deception in
this vision, or cynicism in the king's satisfaction with
it—history is not so simple. The vision was a perfectly
accurate projection of the way Charles saw his realm.
His idealism was politically naive, no doubt, but it was
not hypocritical, and more important, he was not alone

in it. It was consistently supported by the judiciary, and in 1638 the highest court in the land decreed, in the ship-money decision, that prerogative rule was indeed the rule of law. Much of Caroline legal and political history has the quality of a court masque. The darkest moral we are justified in drawing from subsequent events is that if kings will be philosophers, they had better not be Platonists. After a decade of ideals, a disenfranchised Parliament at last declared its authority by virtue of the realities of its power, and the absolute rule of the Stuart monarchy was revealed as a royal charade, a theatrical illusion. Andrew Marvell testifies to the histrionic power of the final act:

> . . . thence the *Royal Actor* born
> The *Tragick Scaffold* might adorn;
>   While round the armed Bands
>   Did clap their bloody hands;
> *He* nothing common did or mean
> Upon that memorable Scene:
>   But with his keener Eye
>   The Axes edge did try:
> Nor call'd the *Gods* with vulgar spight
> To vindicate his helpless Right,
>   But bow'd his comely Head
>   Down, as upon a Bed.[8]

The player king produced, even in Cromwell's loyal retainer, the full Aristotelian measure of admiration, pity, and dread.

[8] "An Horatian Ode upon Cromwell's Return from Ireland," lines 53–64.

Index